Now that I'm retired I think it's time to get on with the important things in life.

Introduction

The purpose of this To-Do List journal is to experience life as you have never before. Use your To-Do lists to challenge yourself and see what new opportunities you can discover. Learn new things about yourself.

As you complete each list, journal your experiences on the adjacent page. Ask yourself questions such as, what did I enjoy most and what did I learn about myself.

There are twelve lists with pre-filled headings to get you started. Create your own personal lists of things you would like to be doing. Stretch your imagination a little and see what ideas you can come up with.

We hope you enjoy this book and get all you can out of each day.

People I would like to reconnect with

Name

Tel

Address

Email

Name

Tel

Address

Email

Name

Tel

Address

Email

Name

Tel

Address

Email

Name

Tel

Address

Email

Name

Tel

Address

Email

Name

Tel

Address

Email

Name

Tel

Address

Email

Places I would like to visit

- [ ]
- [ ]
- [ ]
- [ ]
- [ ]
- [ ]
- [ ]
- [ ]
- [ ]
- [ ]
- [ ]
- [ ]
- [ ]
- [ ]
- [ ]
- [ ]
- [ ]
- [ ]
- [ ]
- [ ]
- [ ]

New skills I would like to learn

- [ ]
- [ ]
- [ ]
- [ ]
- [ ]
- [ ]
- [ ]
- [ ]
- [ ]
- [ ]
- [ ]
- [ ]
- [ ]
- [ ]
- [ ]
- [ ]
- [ ]
- [ ]
- [ ]
- [ ]
- [ ]

Projects I would like to take on

Recipes I would like to try

- [ ]
- [ ]
- [ ]
- [ ]
- [ ]
- [ ]
- [ ]
- [ ]
- [ ]
- [ ]
- [ ]
- [ ]
- [ ]
- [ ]
- [ ]
- [ ]
- [ ]
- [ ]
- [ ]
- [ ]
- [ ]

Things I would like to know more about

- [ ]
- [ ]
- [ ]
- [ ]
- [ ]
- [ ]
- [ ]
- [ ]
- [ ]
- [ ]
- [ ]
- [ ]
- [ ]
- [ ]
- [ ]
- [ ]
- [ ]
- [ ]
- [ ]
- [ ]
- [ ]

Good habits I would like to learn

- [ ] ____
- [ ] ____
- [ ] ____
- [ ] ____
- [ ] ____
- [ ] ____
- [ ] ____
- [ ] ____
- [ ] ____
- [ ] ____
- [ ] ____
- [ ] ____
- [ ] ____
- [ ] ____
- [ ] ____
- [ ] ____
- [ ] ____
- [ ] ____
- [ ] ____
- [ ] ____
- [ ] ____

Bad habits I would like to un-learn

- [ ]
- [ ]
- [ ]
- [ ]
- [ ]
- [ ]
- [ ]
- [ ]
- [ ]
- [ ]
- [ ]
- [ ]
- [ ]
- [ ]
- [ ]
- [ ]
- [ ]
- [ ]
- [ ]
- [ ]
- [ ]

Nutrition habits I would like to start

Fitness habits I would like to start

- [ ] ____________________
- [ ] ____________________
- [ ] ____________________
- [ ] ____________________
- [ ] ____________________
- [ ] ____________________
- [ ] ____________________
- [ ] ____________________
- [ ] ____________________
- [ ] ____________________
- [ ] ____________________
- [ ] ____________________
- [ ] ____________________
- [ ] ____________________
- [ ] ____________________
- [ ] ____________________
- [ ] ____________________
- [ ] ____________________
- [ ] ____________________
- [ ] ____________________
- [ ] ____________________

Books I would like to read

- [ ]
- [ ]
- [ ]
- [ ]
- [ ]
- [ ]
- [ ]
- [ ]
- [ ]
- [ ]
- [ ]
- [ ]
- [ ]
- [ ]
- [ ]
- [ ]
- [ ]
- [ ]
- [ ]
- [ ]
- [ ]

Movies I would like to watch

- [ ] ______
- [ ] ______
- [ ] ______
- [ ] ______
- [ ] ______
- [ ] ______
- [ ] ______
- [ ] ______
- [ ] ______
- [ ] ______
- [ ] ______
- [ ] ______
- [ ] ______
- [ ] ______
- [ ] ______
- [ ] ______
- [ ] ______
- [ ] ______
- [ ] ______
- [ ] ______
- [ ] ______

- [ ]
- [ ]
- [ ]
- [ ]
- [ ]
- [ ]
- [ ]
- [ ]
- [ ]
- [ ]
- [ ]
- [ ]
- [ ]
- [ ]
- [ ]
- [ ]
- [ ]
- [ ]
- [ ]
- [ ]
- [ ]

Printed in Great Britain
by Amazon

85567279R00059